Walking with the Seasons
in Kakadu

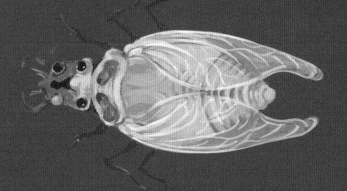

Diane Lucas   Ken Searle

ALLEN&UNWIN

First published in 2003
First published in paperback in 2005

Allen & Unwin
83 Alexander Street
Crows Nest NSW 2065
Australia
Phone: (61 2) 8425 0100
Fax: (61 2) 9906 2218
Email: info@allenandunwin.com
Web: www.allenandunwin.com

National Library of Australia
Cataloguing-in-Publication entry:

Lucas, Diane.
Walking with the seasons in Kakadu.

Includes index.
For Children.
ISBN 978 1 74114 471 0

1. Zoology – Northern Territory – Kakadu National Park –
Pictorial works – Juvenile literature. 2. Plants –
Northern Territory – Kakadu National Park – Pictorial works
– Juvenile literature. 3. Kakadu National Park (N.T.) –
Pictorial works – Juvenile literature. I. Title.

919.4295

Cover and text design by Ken Searle
Set in 14 pt Times by Midland Typesetters, Maryborough, Victoria
This book was printed in December 2017 at CP Printing (Heyuan) Limited at Heyuan
Hi-Tech Development Zone Heyuan, Guangdong Province, P.R.C. Postal Code: 517000.

20 19 18 17 16 15

Teachers' notes for *Walking with the Seasons in Kakadu*, including an orthography to assist with pronunciation, are available from www.allenandunwin.com

Author's note

If you are having trouble pronouncing the names of the seasons,
try sounding them out like this:
Gurrung (*goo-roong*), Gunumeleng (*goo-noo-mel-eng*), Gudjeuk (*goo-jewk*),
Banggerreng (*bung-ger-reng*), Yegge (*yeg-gay*), Wurrgeng (*woor-e-geng*)

Acknowledgements

For the past twenty years, I have been closely associated with Kakadu and the people who live in and look after this country. Gundjeihmi is the language I mostly spoke in Kakadu. The way Aboriginal people share their knowledge with such enthusiasm has enriched and inspired my life, and has encouraged me to write this book.

My great thanks to my family, my Kakadu family and friends and to my great mentors: Ngarduk Ngalbadjan Minnie – (Gapindi), Ruby Ngalmindadjeg, Jessie Alderson, Violet Lawson, Kapirigi, Daisy, Topsy, Gunbunuku, Susan Ngaladjingu, Bluey, Bill Neidje, Dave Lindner and my husband Jeremy. Ian Morris's friendship and his book, *Kakadu*, have been an inspiration. Thanks to Loli, Val, Jillian, Kate, Greg and Aunty Elva for their continual encouragement. I wish to acknowledge my writing mentor, Nadia Wheatley, who has provided me with outstanding critical assistance, and thank her for her very valuable contribution to this book. My sincere thanks also to the Australia Council's Young and Emerging Writers' Initiative for funding the N.T. Writers' Centre 2000 Mentoring Scheme. The staff of the Berry Springs Wildlife Park and Kakadu National Park have been most helpful to Ken and me – thank you.

The paper used in this book is sourced from sustainably managed European forests

For Ngarduk Ngalbadjan Gapindi,
      Wilfrid and Pedro *D.L.*
For Sam and Jess,
      Diane and Jenny *K.S.*

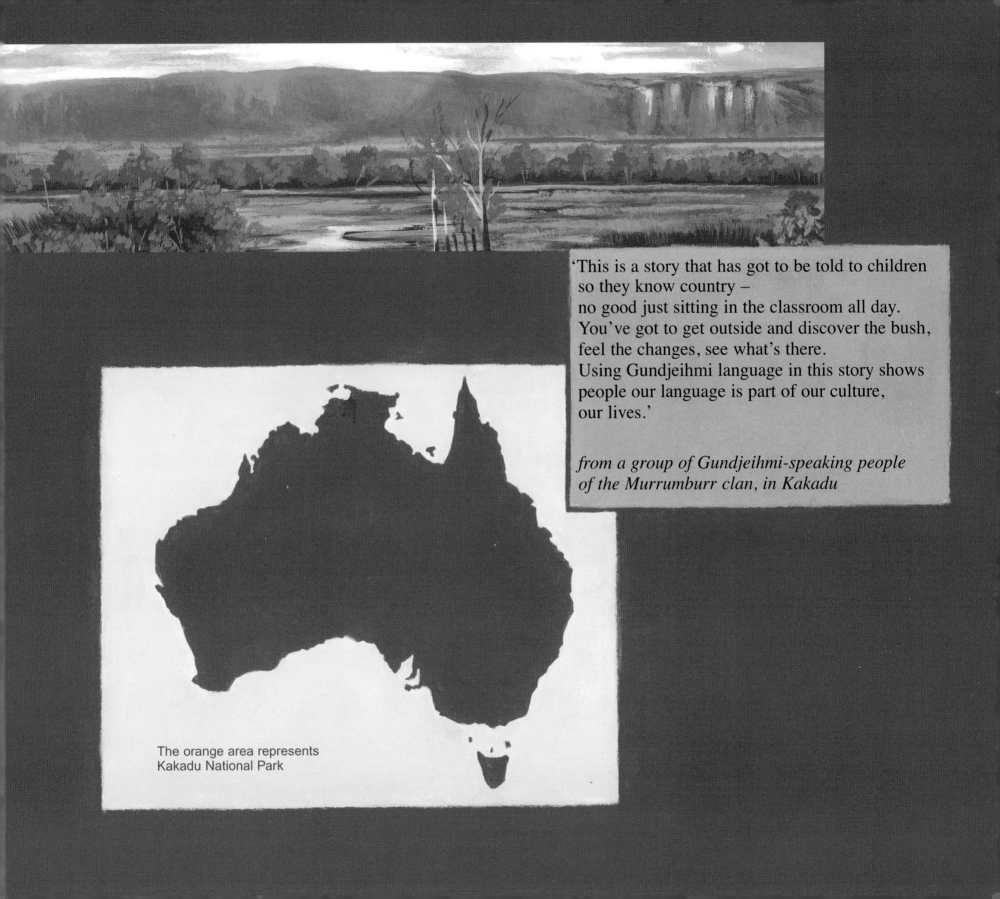

'This is a story that has got to be told to children
so they know country –
no good just sitting in the classroom all day.
You've got to get outside and discover the bush,
feel the changes, see what's there.
Using Gundjeihmi language in this story shows
people our language is part of our culture,
our lives.'

from a group of Gundjeihmi-speaking people
of the Murrumburr clan, in Kakadu

The orange area represents
Kakadu National Park

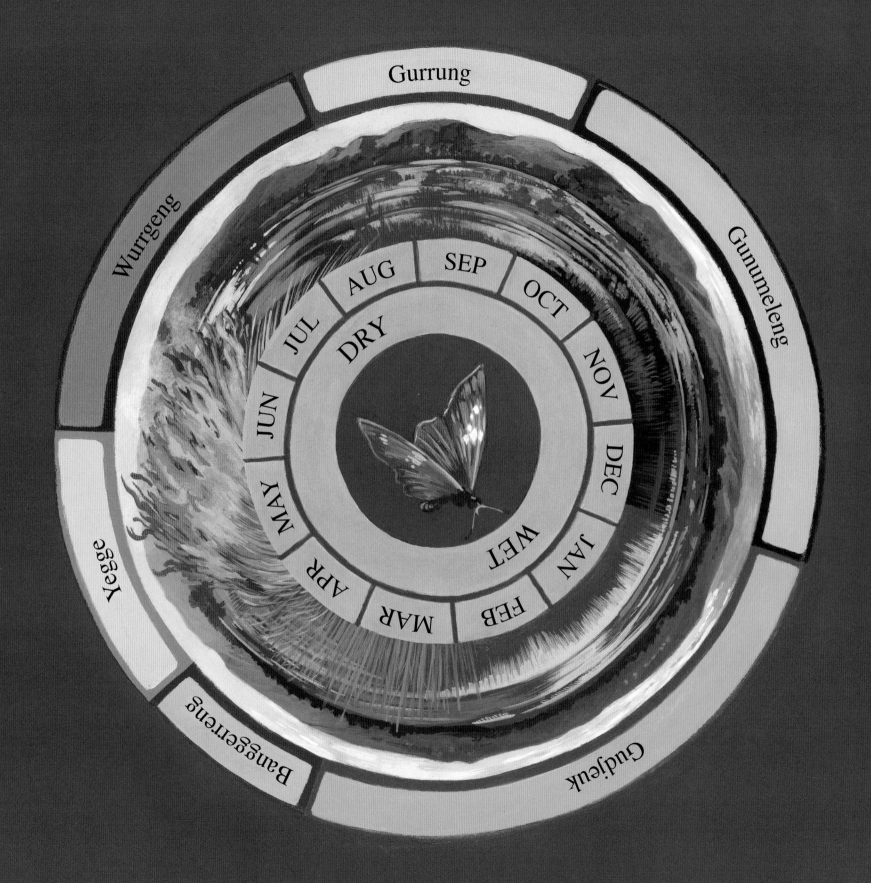

In the Gundjeihmi-speaking people's land in Kakadu,
there are six seasons in the year.

In **Gurrung** we love finding the shells of *dini dini*, cicadas. We put them on our nature table, which we change for every season. The late afternoon wind, *mabilil*, brings the smell of the sea across the land. There are whirly whirly winds, too, which we run and jump into.

In **Gunumeleng** we love watching *Namarrgon*, the lightning man, line up all the clouds in the sky, ready for a storm. This is when his children, *aldjurr*, change their colours. This is also the time when we find shiny red bush apples that lie on the ground, ready for us to eat.

In **Gudjeuk** we love to make shelters out of sheets of paperbark. We eat the luscious red fruit of *anmamdak*, the canthium plum. When night falls, we like to watch the glow beetles dance in the darkness, or lie in our beds and listen to the drumming of the rain.

In **Banggerreng** we love to walk through the spear grass looking for the hiding yam vines so we can dig them up to cook. This is the time when the tall spear grass falls over from the knock 'em down storms. It is fun to make cubbyhouses with bundles of grass before the fires come and eat them up.

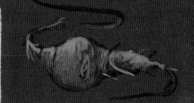

In **Yegge** we love to swim among the waterlilies in the lagoon, and nibble on their seeds. This is the dry season, when the wind blows the fires across the land, cleaning away the old grass and fallen branches. As we walk through the bush, we chew on the fat billygoat plums.

In **Wurrgeng** we love to huddle around the campfire on the cold nights, under a sky full of bright stars. We listen to the wind blowing through the trees, and we hear *gordol*, the grass owls, calling. We make up our own songs about the bush and the seasons. Soon it will be **Gurrung** again!

GURRUNG

Around the middle of August,
Gurrung begins.
This is the dry hot season,
yet early mornings can bring mist.
As the days move along,
the ground gets hot,
the sand gets hot,
the stones get hot.
Leaf rain falls from some of the trees.
In the early evening,
mabilil, the sea-water wind,
blows across the land,
bringing relief from the heat of the day.
Nardjulum, the whirly-whirly winds,
can carry fire across the land,
over the floodplains,
and through the woodlands.

Ngangalad, frill-necked lizards,
hunt in the sun, and rest, clinging to trees.

When it is hot and dry,
almangiyi, the long-necked turtle,
buries into the mud on the floodplain
to sleep.

Anggung, honey from native bees,
is rich now. The bees have been busy
carrying all the nectar and pollen
from the flowers.

Merlemerle, butterflies,
and *waleddon*, shield bugs,
find moist shady places
to shelter in the jungle.

Dini dini, the cicadas,
have left their shells everywhere.
They have walked out of their old shells,
to grow new ones that fit.

Andjeermain, kurrajong,
brightens the bush with its red flowers.
The blossoms give nectar
to bees and many birds.

Andudjmi, the green plum tree,
andak, the yellow plum tree,
andjarduk, the big red apple tree –
are all bursting into flower.
They make us think
of the lovely fruits that will form
during October and November,
and be ready to eat in December.

Andjed, the kapok fruits,
are big and green.
Their fluff is forming in the pods.
When they pop,
it is a sign that the eggs of *gumugen*,
the freshwater crocodiles,
are hatching.

Angol, the cocky apple tree,
is busy making blossoms.
Each morning, a carpet of flowers
surrounds the trees.
The hawk moths and bats
have come in the night
to gather the nectar.

Every season we make a nature table.
As we walk around in the bush
we collect things to put on our nature table.
These things grow a seasonal story.

Gurrung Nature Table
On our nature table this season we have collected:

shells of *dini dini* (cicadas)
shell of *almangiyi* (long-necked turtle)
popped fruits and green pods of *andjed* (kapok tree)
red flowers of *andjeermain* (kurrajong tree)
pods of *andjalen* (woolly butt eucalypt tree)

feathers of *garnamarr* (red-tailed black cockatoos)
feathers of *bamurru* (magpie geese)
some *gunworrg* (coloured leaves)
pieces of wings of *merlemerle* (butterflies)
clay models of *ngangalad* (frill-necked lizards)

Minbulung, Torres Strait pigeons, eat the Carpentaria palm seeds.

Garnamarr, the red-tailed black cockatoos, crunch on eucalypt seeds.

Magagurr, the pelicans, glide across the water in search of food. Their large beaks scoop up fish and water as they hunt across the floodplain.

Djurrbiyuk, the whistle ducks, huddle together chattering on the muddy banks. When they fly, their wings make a whistling noise.

Bamurru, the magpie geese, feed on lily flowers and lily roots, and the bulbs of rush grass. Look at them! Tail and feet in the air, as they feed.

We celebrate with Mother Earth the hot dry months of *Gurrung*. As the floodplain dries out, the waterbirds gather to feed and live near the remaining pools. Trees of the woodland flower and fruit. Earth hot, sun bright, leaves fall like rain… Now it's *Gurrung* we cool off in the billabong.

Algordoh, the brolga, quietly walks around picking at lily roots, fish and plants.

GUNUMELENG

It is the season of *Gunumeleng*,
the time that storms are upon the land.
Namarrgon, the lightning man,
emerges from the rocks, into the sky.
The clouds burst, rain falls.
This brings rich growth to the dry country.
Barrmarrdja, the wind from the west,
starts to blow.
The months of dry have finished.

The mother *ginga*, saltwater crocodile,
makes her nest on the river bank.
A mound of mud and grass
holds a clutch of crocodile eggs.

In the heat of the day,
nawandak, the file snake,
hides in holes among the tree roots
under the water.

When a storm falls,
djadi, the frog, sits on a rock.
Singing loudly, he bathes in the rain,
calling out to a mate.

During the day, *dini dini*, cicadas,
fill the air with their song.
When darkness falls,
garrdidi, crickets, take their place.

Ngangalad, the frill-necked lizard,
stands tall,
flanging his collar of colours.

Aldjurr, Leichhardt's grasshoppers,
stand out brightly in the bush.
They sit and feed on the plant, *warrumba*.
Gundjeihmi-speaking people call these
grasshoppers '*Namarrgon's* children' because
they moult and transform into their
new colours when the storms return.

Andudjmi, the green plum,
tastes sweet and tangy,
a bit like the juice of passionfruit.
We like shaking the tree
to watch the fruits fall.

Andjalbirru, the pink apple,
has large pink fruits that hang
like Christmas decorations.
They taste sweet, like guava apples.

Andak, the yellow milky plum,
has a hard skin.
When you bite it – out pops a seed
covered with stringy flesh
that you suck.
It tastes like mango.

Andjarduk, the red apples,
fall to the ground.
If they are soft, they are ready to bite.
The flesh makes your mouth tingle,
with a tart flavour, a taste like cloves.

This is the season when *Namarrgon*
comes out of his cave
bringing lightning and thunder across the land.
His children, *aldjurr*,
change colour at this time.

Gunumeleng Nature Table
On our nature table this season we have:

a clay bowl with fruits of *andudjmi* (green plums)
a dish with fruits of *andak* (yellow milky plums)
a basket with fruits of *andjarduk* (red apple)
a basket with fruits of *andjalbirru* (pink apple)
beeswax puppets of *aldjurr* (Leichhardt's grasshopper)
clay models of *ngangalad* (frill-necked lizards)

shells of *dini dini* (cicadas)
clay models of *nawandak* (file snakes)
a nest of grass and mud for mother *ginga* (saltwater crocodile)
felt puppets of *djadi* (frogs)
flowers of *andjiladjila* (crinum lilies)
flowers of *gamaang* (yams)

Mayhmayh, the shining flycatcher
nests in a tree, over the creek.
From her small, rounded nest of mud
she can fly off to
catch insects to eat.

Djawok, the storm bird,
is a large black bird with a wailing song
that can be heard echoing through the forest,
as it calls for a mate.

Dawhdaw, dollar birds,
glide on wind currents,
catching insects, especially cicadas.
As they fly, you can see a large white
dot, like a dollar, on each wing.
Their call is more of a squawk
than a song.

Bukbuk, pheasant coucals,
have long tails that seem to make
them stagger as they fly.
Now the rain is here,
they have a haunting song
that sounds like a drum-roll.

When the rains wet the earth,
the bulbs under the ground sprout up.
Walking amongst the woodlands,
we find bush fruits ripening.
It's a time to celebrate the harvest.
The sweet green plums,
the milky yellow plums,
the red apples, the pink apples –
plenty for all to taste.

GUDJEUK

Gudjeuk is monsoon season –
an exciting time of year.
It starts around Christmas time.
Early storms move the water
across the land.
Creeks start flowing
and new plant and animal life emerges.
Barra, the north-west monsoon winds,
bring rain, rain, rain.
The land gets filled up with water.
From the rock country the water falls,
and flows down to the creeks,
across the floodplain,
into the rivers, and to the sea.
Everything is moving along,
feasting and growing.
Lots of animals, birds, insects and plants
have their babies at this time of year.

Ginga, the saltwater crocodile,
watches as her eggs hatch and the
babies move to the water to feed.

Djadi, the frogs, sing with the rain,
and spread their eggs in all the water.
Djadi is food for many animals and birds.
Nawandak, the file snake, eats plenty of them.

Now the floodwaters have forced
murlbu, the dusky rats,
out of their holes on the floodplain.
Boloko, the water python,
feasts on them.

There is a story an old Aboriginal woman told us
about *gurrih*, the blue-tongue lizard,
and *annyunyek*, the wild grape vine.
'When that *annyunyek* is flowering,
gurrih is having her babies.
When that *annyunyek* is fruiting,
that tells us the lizards are fat and ready to eat.'

Anboiberre, bush apple trees,
grow along the banks of creeks.
They are a strong, solid tree
and their leaves hang over the water.
When the white fruits fall,
many wash downstream.
They are eaten by
dunbukmang, black bream, and
ngardehwor, the short-necked turtle.
We also like to eat
these large white apples.
They taste spicy and floury.

Birriyalang, the big, tall paperbarks,
grow along the creeks. When it rains,
they are covered with white flowers.
The thick scent fills the night air,
bringing *guluban*, flying fox,
to feast upon the nectar.
Some women in Arnhem Land tell stories
about how *gurruk*, freshwater mussels,
get fat in the night
when they fly up out of the water
to eat the nectar of these blossoms.

Anbedje, spear grass,
seems to grow while we watch it.
The green spears surround us
as we walk through woodland country.

Anmamdak, canthium plum,
is a luscious red squashy fruit.
This small tree grows along creeks.
Many birds like these fruits too.

We collect sheets of bark
from the paperbark tree,
to build a shelter.
Then we make a little fire.
Now we feel like a snack
so we walk along
looking for some bush potatoes.
'Badju, badju, badju,' we sing.
When we find their flower
nodding in the grass,
we dig up the badju yams
and eat them raw,
or roast them on hot coals.

Gudjeuk Nature Table
On our nature table this season we have:

a basket of andjarduk (red apple) fruits
a bowl of anboiberre (white apple) fruits
a clay dish of andudjmi (green plums)
fruits from the anmamdak (canthium plum)
flowers from the birriyalang (paperbark trees)
flowers of the anganggi (freshwater mangrove trees)
feathers of bukbuk (pheasant coucal)
a bowl of badju (potato yams or bush potatoes)
a clay model of gurrih (blue-tongue lizard)

a piece of the annyunyek (native grape vine)
clay models of boloko (water pythons)
felt puppets of djadi (frogs)
clay models of ginga nesting (saltwater crocodiles)
clay models of bamurru nesting (magpie geese)
flowers and fruits of adjinakadj (arrowroot)
felt puppets of walburr (glow beetles)
coloured barks
shiny green leaves

Djeriddird, azure kingfishers,
make their nests in a tunnel
away from the flooded creeks.
They find plenty of insect tucker
to feed their babies.
We usually hear these birds
before we see them.
They give a high-pitched whistle
which alerts us.
Then we see a flash of blue-brown,
just above the water,
as a single bird flies by.

Berred berred, the rainbow bee-eaters,
have a wonderful feast
on the many insects that breed during
this hot, humid wet season of *Gudjeuk*.
They make a sound like a cricket calling.

Bamurru, the magpie geese,
look for nesting places
on the floodplain.
Towards the end of *Gudjeuk*,
they make their grassy nests
close to each other.
The gathering of thousands of geese,
chattering loudly, is like a wave of music
rolling across the plain.

We celebrate *Gudjeuk*.
Blue-grey skies burst with rain.
Bush food trees give plenty of fruits.
The yams in the earth are swelling.
As they grow,
they send more and more leaves
to twine around trees.
The country is green, green, green,
and bursting with water.
Many birds and animals are nesting
now there is an abundance of tucker.
At night, *walburr*, the glow beetles,
fly through the darkness
making magical patterns,
as they search for a mate.
Wind blows, water flows,
streams fill, fish swim
and children sing…

BANGGERRENG

Djimurru, the wind that blows from the south-east, comes at the beginning of the season of *Banggerreng*. Wild rain, known as *nagul*, comes later in this season. It tells us that the last storms of the wet season are here, the knock 'em down storms.
These storms flatten the tall, yellowing spear grass. Their seeds spiral into the ground, like corkscrews. Here they sit, waiting in the earth for the storms that will come with the return of the *Gunumeleng* season. As floodwaters drop, the harvest time begins for all.

Colourful *galangarridjgalangarridj*, dragonflies of gold and brown, dart around catching insects. They tell us it is *Banggerreng* time.

The calls of the *dini dini*, cicadas, fade away, as they die off at this time.

Yamidj, the green katydid insect, calls from the spear grass, telling us the yams are ready to dig.

Annyunyek, the native grape, is fruiting. This tells us that *gurrih*, the blue-tongue lizards, have had their babies.

The name '*bourd*' is used for both a green pod and a fish. The green pod attaches to a spear grass flower, and hangs like a cocoon. When you find one, you can break off the pod and blow the black powdery dust to the wind. Gundjeihmi-speaking people say this is a way of making the *bourd* fish grow fat.

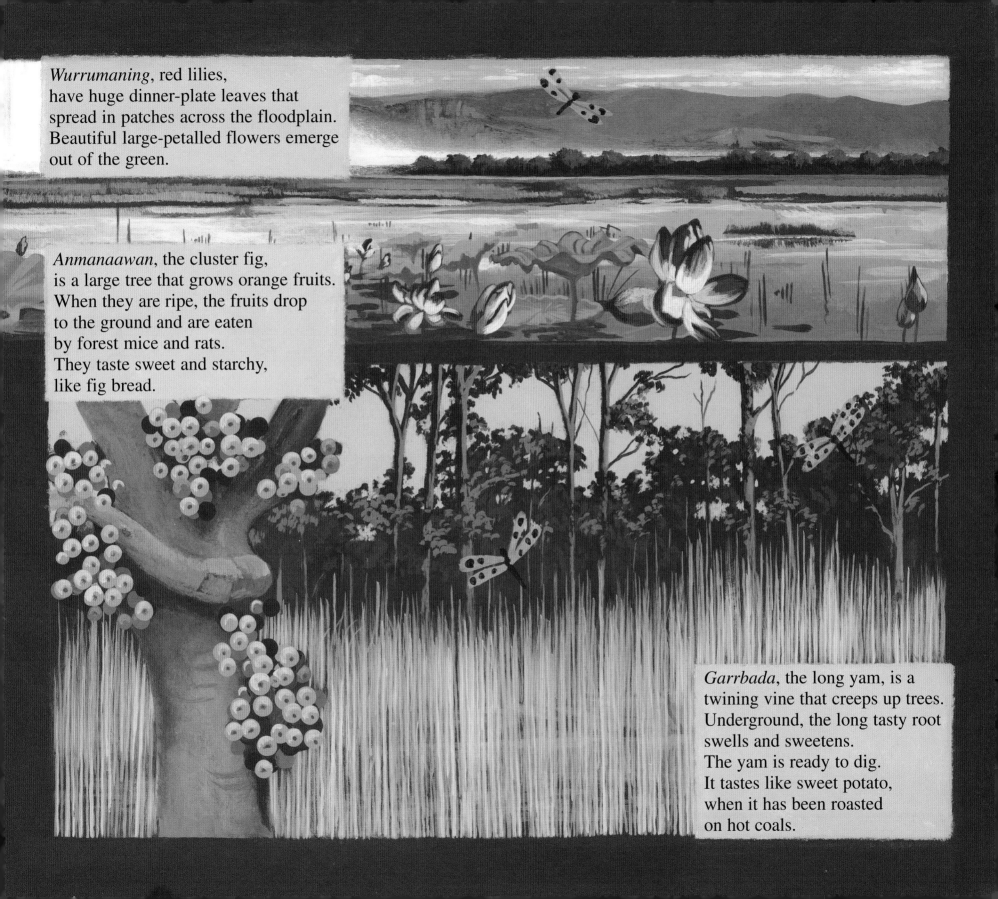

Wurrumaning, red lilies,
have huge dinner-plate leaves that
spread in patches across the floodplain.
Beautiful large-petalled flowers emerge
out of the green.

Anmanaawan, the cluster fig,
is a large tree that grows orange fruits.
When they are ripe, the fruits drop
to the ground and are eaten
by forest mice and rats.
They taste sweet and starchy,
like fig bread.

Garrbada, the long yam, is a
twining vine that creeps up trees.
Underground, the long tasty root
swells and sweetens.
The yam is ready to dig.
It tastes like sweet potato,
when it has been roasted
on hot coals.

Anbulubi, *anwourbmi*, *angulahbang*
are some of the woodland yams ready to dig.
They are like morning tea snacks,
to keep us cheerful.
These plants have a root like a carrot or potato.
They hide really well among the spear grass,
but once you find them, they are easy to dig.
We lightly roast them on coals.
They taste delicious, like sweet potatoes.

Banggerreng Nature Table
On our nature table this season we have:

flowers of *andjirrwirr* (wattle tree)
clay models of *bourd* (fish)
felt finger puppets of *galangarridjgalangarridj* (dragonflies)
a basket of ripe orange fruits of *andjimdjim* (pandanus)
stems of flowering and seeding *anbedje* (spear grass)
a clay bowl of fruits from *annyunyek* (native grape vine)
some clay models of *garrbada* (long yams)

a dish of ripe fruits from *anmanaawan* (bush fig)
felt flowers of *wurrumaning* (red lilies)
a stem of fruits from *angulurrudj* (sand palm)
a grassy nest for clay-modelled *raagul* (red-eyed partridge pigeon)
clay models of parent and baby *algordoh* (brolgas)
a grassy nest with clay models of eggs and baby *bamurru* (magpie geese)
felt puppets of fat *loklok* (skinks)

Raagul, the red-eyed pigeon,
makes her nest
in the lowland forests
among the grass and leaves.
She will sit and hatch her egg
while there is plenty of grass seed
for her baby to feed on.

Now floodwaters have dropped,
the nests of *bamurru*, the magpie geese,
sit among the wild rice
and water chestnut reeds.
There is plenty of tucker here
as their babies are hatching.

Algordoh, the brolga chicks,
have hatched from their nests
made from reeds on the floodplain.
Now they stalk along with their parents
in the shallow waters,
feeding on plants and insects.

In the night, you can hear
a quiet humming call from *djurrul*,
the tawny frogmouth.
Then, in a flash, down she swoops
to catch one of the many insects
that have appeared over the wet season.

As the rain eases,
the floodplain water levels go down.
Animals, birds, insects and people
all celebrate *Banggerreng*
by feasting in the bush gardens
that have grown during the wet months.
The trees stand tall against blue sky,
barks of yellow and grey.
Their leaves are fresh, bright green
from the many months of rain.
Listen to the wind
Listen to the wind
Listen to the wind in the trees…

YEGGE

The dry season of *Yegge* arrives with *djimurru*,
the strong wind blowing from the south-east.
It is often said by the local people,
'This wind, blow away the water.'
Yegge is the season for much burning.
The fires eat up
the fallen spear grass.
In the wake of the fire,
animals and birds come out
to catch insects and other creatures
running from the flames.
There is a smoky haze in the air
for much of the day.
The fires usually die out by evening
with the cooler air blowing north from
the winter season of southern Australia.

An old Aboriginal man said,
'In old generation way,
we burnim that grass in *Yegge*
and cleanim more in *Wurrgeng*.
That fire he won't hurt …
good for that grass coming up
and all the animals.'

When the fires come,
yok, the brown bandicoot,
often finds his grass camp burning.
He needs to run to the edge of the fire,
or onto ground already burnt,
so his feet don't get sizzled.
Here he will also find insects to eat.

Almangiyi, the long-necked turtle,
is feasting on frogs, fish, beetles, tadpoles.
She is fattening up,
so she will be ready to lay her eggs
during the next season.

The woodlands are splashed with yellow
now the wattle flowers blossom.
Andjoh is one of the many wattles
flowering at this time.
Godjong, the witchetty grubs, like to eat
the insides of these trees,
so *andjoh* only have a short life.

Andjalen, the woolly butt tree,
begins to flower in *Yegge*.
This common woodland eucalypt
hums with the songs of birds and bees which
are attracted to the scented orange flowers.
When these trees finish flowering at the end
of *Wurrgeng*, the Gundjeihmi-speaking
people know to finish burning.

Anmorlak, the billygoat plums, are fat now.
They are dropping to the ground.
It is time to eat these fruits.
They taste sweet and sour,
and you can chew on them for a while
as you walk along in the bush.
When you are ready for another one,
you will probably have reached
another tree.

When *anbaandarr*, the turkey bush trees,
are covered with star-shaped pink flowers,
they tell us that *Yegge* is here.
Wallabies and bower birds like to camp
in the shade of these small trees.

The flowers of *andem*, waterlilies,
seem to cover the floodplains,
and their strong fragrance fills the air.
The purple-tinged flowers stand among
flat green leaves, which make a platform
for the small lotus lily birds,
garrdagoiyengoiyen, to live.
Dragonflies dart above them, bees nuzzle
into their nectar, the sun shines upon them.
Turtles and fish swim under their leaves.
Waterlilies float in the sun.
Waterlilies blow with the breeze.

Yegge Nature Table
On our nature table this season we have:

flowers of *anbaandarr* (turkey bush)
flowers of *andjoh* (wattle tree)
felt flowers of *andem, mardjakalang*, (waterlilies)
flowers of *andjalen* (woolly butt eucalypt tree)
flowers of *andjandjek* (grevillea)
seeds of *anbedje* (spear grass)
felt puppets of *garnamarr* (red-tailed black cockatoos)
clay models of *gornobolo* (agile wallabies)
clay models of *yok* (brown bandicoots)

felt puppets of *ngarradj* (sulphur-crested cockatoos)
clay models of *loklok* (rainbow skinks)
felt puppets of *galangarridjgalangarridj* (dragonflies)
felt puppets of *nawurrgbil* (whistling kites)
clay models of *murlbu* (dusky rats)
clay bowl of fruits from *anmorlak* (billygoat plum)
felt puppet of *yamidj* (green katydid)
clay models of *almangiyi* (long-necked turtle)

Nawurrgbil, the whistling kites,
follow the fire to catch
skinks, grasshoppers, mice
and dragon lizards,
who are running from the flames.

Berred berred, the rainbow bee-eaters,
perch high on deciduous trees
where they have a good view
of passing dragonflies.

After a fire, *garnamarr*,
the red-tailed black cockatoos,
are well camouflaged
as they feast on the ground,
on the seeds that have fallen
from the spear grass.

Ngarradj, sulphur-crested cockatoos,
can be seen in large groups
at the edge of the floodplains,
in the tall paperbark trees.
They squawk and screech,
as they preen themselves,
or hang upside down on branches,
like acrobatic clowns.

We celebrate the dry weather
when the woodlands blossom,
and the floodplains are covered
with fragrant lilies.
When fires are burning
the old grasses make way for new growth.
There are fruits and nectar, yams, seeds
and insects for everyone to feast upon.

WURRGENG

The dry season days of *Wurrgeng*
begin with cool mornings.
Gunmaiyorrk wind blows up lightly
from the south-east during the morning
and can blow until late afternoon.
The trees have many songs
as the wind blows through their leaves.
Seasonal creeks are drying up,
yet the floodplains still have lots of water.
The flowering waterlilies
across the floodplains
are visited by many birds,
insects, and even people.

Gumugen, the freshwater crocodile,
lays her eggs on a sandy bank near the creek.
The eggs will incubate in the warm sand
before hatching.

Gowarrang, the echidna, is a shy animal
who hides away in caves and rocks.
If you are out at night, you might see him
hunting for ants and termites,
often amongst the spinifex grass.
Gowarrang are breeding now.

Ngyangma, the quoll, lives in the forest.
The mother may be seen
carrying three or more babies on her back,
as she hunts in the night
for insects or skinks or nesting birds.

Gardab, the orb spider,
spins a beautiful golden web.
She is a large spider who lives in the jungle.
When you go near her web, she bounces gently,
warning you to tread with care.
She is a sort of guardian of the forest.

The blue quandong, *yirrlalal*,
is a magic lantern tree covered
with white flowers. Now it has
translucent blue fruits that taste
starchy and tangy.

Andjandjek, the grevillea,
has large orange flowers
that hang like a coral garden
and drip with rich honey nectar,
attracting birds, bees and people.

Anrebel, the stringybark eucalypt,
only flowers during *Wurrgeng*.
This nectar adds to the feast
for the many birds visiting these trees.

Andjed, the kapok trees
are small and spread widely across
the woodlands and rock country.
Around the month of June,
they lose their leaves and stand brightly
clothed with large yellow flowers.

Angindjek and *garrbada* are two yams.
Their roots are ready to dig now.
Angindjek is easy to dig,
but needs to be prepared the proper way,
washing away the 'cheekiness',
before it can be eaten.
Garrbada takes time to dig,
but it can be roasted or boiled
without any special preparation.
These yams are eaten in the same way
as rice, pasta and bread.

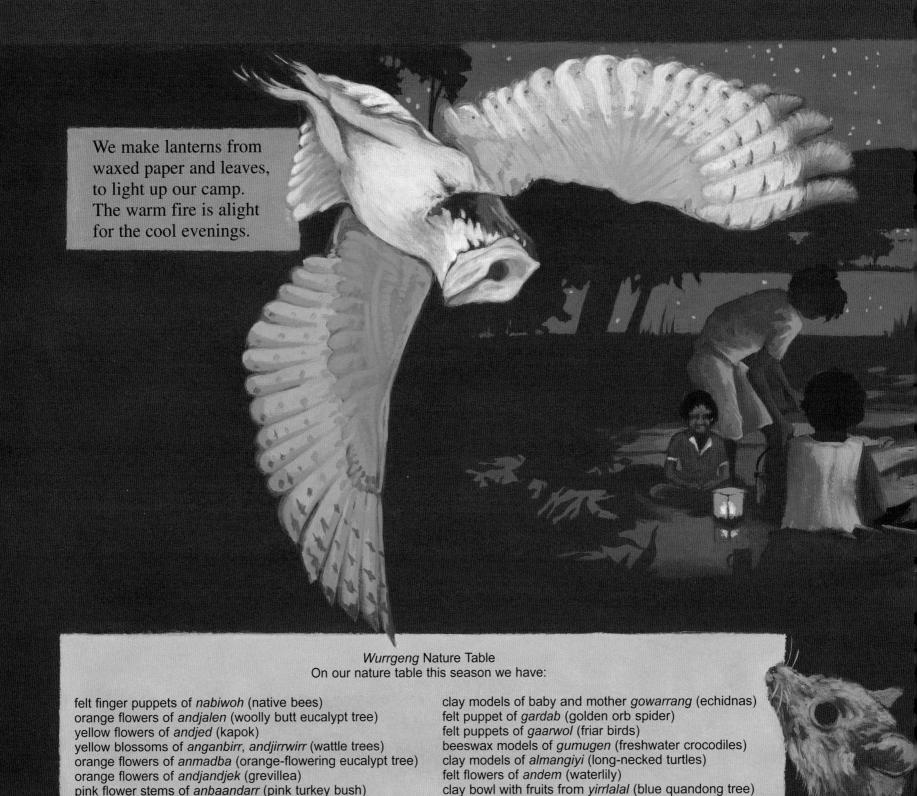

We make lanterns from
waxed paper and leaves,
to light up our camp.
The warm fire is alight
for the cool evenings.

Wurrgeng Nature Table
On our nature table this season we have:

felt finger puppets of *nabiwoh* (native bees)
orange flowers of *andjalen* (woolly butt eucalypt tree)
yellow flowers of *andjed* (kapok)
yellow blossoms of *anganbirr, andjirrwirr* (wattle trees)
orange flowers of *anmadba* (orange-flowering eucalypt tree)
orange flowers of *andjandjek* (grevillea)
pink flower stems of *anbaandarr* (pink turkey bush)

clay models of baby and mother *gowarrang* (echidnas)
felt puppet of *gardab* (golden orb spider)
felt puppets of *gaarwol* (friar birds)
beeswax models of *gumugen* (freshwater crocodiles)
clay models of *almangiyi* (long-necked turtles)
felt flowers of *andem* (waterlily)
clay bowl with fruits from *yirrlalal* (blue quandong tree)

At night, out on the floodplain,
you can hear *gordol*, the grass owls, calling.
They are out to catch *murlbu*, the dusky rats.

Gaarwol, friar birds,
are busy gathering nectar
from the flowering eucalypt trees.
Their calls are loud and they sound so happy
as they chatter in the bush.

The male *djuwe*, bower bird,
is decorating his bower
with collected treasures from the bush.
He is busy attracting a female to his home.

Garragan, the brown falcon,
is keenly following the smoke to catch lizards
and other animals running from the flames.
This bird is known
to Gundjeihmi-speaking people
as 'fire carrier' – the bird that carries burning
sticks to start more fires.

This is the time of dazzling blue skies,
and cool, crystal-clear nights.
We celebrate *Wurrgeng*
by sitting around our campfire
under a sky full of bright stars.

Now that *Wurrgeng* is over,
it is time again for *Gurrung* –
the dry hot season.
As the days move along,
the ground gets hot,
the sand gets hot,
the stones get hot.
Leaf rain falls from some of the trees.
In the early evening,
mabilil, the sea-water wind,
blows across the land,
bringing relief from the heat of the day.

Dini dini, the cicadas,
have left their shells everywhere.
They have walked out
of their old shells,
to grow new ones that fit.

We too are growing, changing,
as the world turns,
and the cycle goes on …

Through the seasons we wander –
looking, learning, smelling, eating,
playing in the bush,
and watching the changes
to the country around us.

GLOSSARY AND INDEX

adjinakadj [16] — arrowroot (*Tacca leontopetaloides*)
aldjurr [10, 12] — Leichhardt's grasshopper (*Petasida ephippigera*)
algordoh [9, 20, 21] — brolga (*Grus rubindicus*)
almangiyi [6, 8, 22, 24, 28] — northern long-necked turtle (*Chelodina rugosa*)
anbaandarr [23, 24, 28] — turkey bush (*Calytrix exstipulata*)
anbedje [15, 20, 24] — spear grass (*Sorghum intrans*)
anboiberre [15, 16] — white apple tree (*Syzygium forte*)
anbulubi [20] — type of yam (*Eriosema chinense*)
andak [7, 11, 12] — yellow plum tree (*Persoonia falcata*)
andem [24, 28] — waterlily (*Nymphaea violacea*)
andjalbirru [11, 12] — pink apple tree (*Syzygium euc.spp.blesseri*)
andjalen [8, 23, 24, 28] — woolly butt eucalypt tree (*Eucalyptus miniata*)
andjandjek [24, 27, 28] — grevillea (*Grevillea pteridifolia*)
andjarduk [7, 11, 12, 16] — red apple tree (*Syzygium suborbiculare*)
andjed [7, 8, 27, 28] — kapok tree (*Cochlospermum fraseri*)
andjeermain [7, 8] — kurrajong (*Brachychiton megaphyllus*)
andjiladjila [12] — crinum lily (*Crinum angustifolium*)
andjimdjim [20] — pandanus (*Pandanus aquaticus*)
andjirrwirr [20, 28] — a type of wattle (*Acacia aulacocarpa*)
andjoh [23, 24] — a type of wattle (*Acacia difficilis*)
andudjmi [7, 11, 12, 16] — green plum tree (*Buchanania obovata*)
anganbirr [28] — a type of wattle (*Acacia oncinocarpa*)
ananggi [16] — freshwater mangrove tree (*Barringtonia acutangula*)
anggung [6] — bush honey
angulahbang [20] — a type of yam (*Austrodolichos errabundus*)
angulurrudj [20] — sand palm (*Livistona humilis*)
angindjek [27] — a type of yam (*Dioscorea bulbifera*)
angol [7] — cocky apple tree (*Planchonia careya*)
anmadba [28] — orange-flowering eucalypt (*Eucalyptus phoenecia*)
anmamdak [5, 15, 16] — canthium plum (*Canthium schultzeii*)
anmanaawan [19, 20] — cluster fig (bush fig) (*Ficus racemosa*)
anmorlak [23, 24] — billygoat plum tree (*Terminalia ferdinandiana*)
annyunyek [14, 16, 18, 20] — wild grape vine (*Ampelocissus acetosa*)
anrebel [27] — stringybark eucalypt (*Eucalyptus tetrodonta*)
anwourbmi [20] — type of yam (*Ipomoea graminea*)
badju [16] — yam – bush potato (*Brachystelma glabriflorum*)
bamurru [8, 9, 16, 17, 20, 21] — magpie goose (*Anseranas semipalmata*)
barra [14] — north-west monsoon wind
barrmarrdja [10] — wind that blows from the west
berred berred [17, 25] — rainbow bee-eater (*Merops ornatus*)
birriyalang [15, 16] — paperbark tree (*Melaleuca leucadendra*)
boloko [14, 16] — water python (*Liasis fuscus*)
bourd [18, 20] — green pod; type of fish (*Leoiotherapon unicolor*)
bukbuk [13, 16] — pheasant coucal (*Centropus phasianinus*)
dawhdaw [13] — dollar bird (*Eurystomus orientalis*)
dini dini [5, 6, 8, 10, 12, 18, 30] — cicada (*Thorpha sessiliba distant*)
djadi [10, 12, 14, 16] — frog (*Litoria rothii, Litoria caerulea*)
djawok [13] — storm bird (*Eudynamis scolopacea*)
djeriddird [17] — azure kingfisher (*Ceyx azurea*)
djimurru [18, 22] — wind that blows from the south-east

djurrbiyuk [9] — plumed whistling duck (*Dendrocygna eytoni*)
djurrul [21] — tawny frogmouth (*Podargus strigoides*)
djuwe [29] — great bower bird (*Chlamydera nuchalis*)
dunbukmang [15] — black bream (*Hephaestus fuliginosus*)
gaarwol [28, 29] — friar bird (*Philemon argenticeps*)
galangarridjgalangarridj [18, 20, 24] — dragonfly (*Family: Odonata*)
gamaang [12] — yam (*Amorphophallus paeonifolius*)
gardab [26, 28] — golden orb spider (*Nephila insignis*)
garnamarr [8, 9, 24, 25] — red-tailed black cockatoo (*Calyptorhynchus magnificus*)
garragan [29] — brown falcon (*Falco berigora*)
garrbada [19, 20, 27] — a type of long yam (*Dioscorea transversa*)
garrdagoiyengoiyen [24] — lotus lily bird (*Irediparra gallinacea*)
garrdidi [10] — cricket (*Order: Orthoptera*)
ginga [10, 12, 14, 16] — saltwater crocodile (*Crocodylus porosus*)
godjong [23] — witchetty grub
gordol [5, 29] — eastern grass owl (*Tyto longimembris*)
gornobolo [24] — agile wallaby (*Macropus agilis*)
gowarrang [26, 28] — echidna (*Tachyglossus aculeatus*)
guluban [15] — red flying fox (*Pteropus scapulatus*)
gumugen [7, 26, 28] — freshwater crocodile (*Crocodylus johnstoni*)
gunmaiyorrk [26] — wind that blows from the south-east
gunworrg [8] — leaves
gurrih [14, 16, 18] — blue-tongue lizard (*Tiliqua scincoides*)
gurruk [15] — freshwater mussel (*Velesunio angasi*)
loklok [20, 24] — any kind of skink (*Ctenotus robustus, essingtoni*)
mabilil [5, 6, 30] — wind that comes from the sea
magagurr [9] — pelican (*Pelecanus conspicillatus*)
mardjakalang [24] — waterlily (*Nymphaea macrosperma*)
mayhmayh [13] — shining flycatcher (*Myiagra alecto*)
merlemerle [6, 8] — butterfly (*Polyura pyrrhus, Graphium eurypylus*)
minbulung [9, 13] — Torres Strait pigeon (*Ducula spilorrhoa*)
murlbu [14, 24, 29] — dusky rat (*Rattus tunneyi*)
nabiwoh [28] — native bee (*Trigona sp.*)
nagul [18] — wild rain
Namarrgon [5, 10, 12] — the lightning man
nardjulum [6] — whirly-whirly wind
nawandak [10, 12, 14] — file snake (*Acrochordus arafurae*)
nawurrgbil [24, 25] — whistling kite (*Haliastur sphenurus*)
ngangalad [6, 8, 10, 12] — frill-necked lizard (*Chlamydosaurus kingii*)
ngardehwor [15] — short-necked turtle (*Emydura victoriae*)
ngarradj [24, 25] — sulphur-crested cockatoo (*Cacatua galerita*)
ngyangma [26] — northern quoll (*Dasyurus hallucatus*)
raagul [20, 21] — red-eyed partridge pigeon (*Geophaps smithii*)
walburr [16, 17] — glow beetle
waleddon [6] — shield bug (*Lampromicra senator*)
warrumba [10] — plant for Leichhardt's grasshopper (*Pityrodia jamesii*)
wurrumaning [19, 20] — red lily (*Nelumbo nucifera*)
yamidj [18, 24] — green katydid insect
yirrlalal [27, 28] — blue quandong tree (*Elaeocarpus arnhemicus*)
yok [22, 24] — northern brown bandicoot (*Isoodon macrourus*)